TO DIE IN LATIN

To Die In Latin

poems by
William Ryan

Lynx House Press
Amherst, Massachusetts / Portland, Oregon

ACKNOWLEDGEMENTS

Some of the poems in this volume have been previously published in periodicals as follows:

Red Dirt: "Not to Make Emptiness a Point of View," "C&W" (under the title "Blues")

"Not to Make Emptiness a Point of View," "C&W," "Prayer for the Dead," "Give It Up," "The Solo You Took on a Solo of Mine," and "Tropism in Religious Painting in the Prado," appeared in the limited edition volume, *Not To Make Emptiness A Point Of View* (Oat City Press, Tuscaloosa, AL), 1991.

Library of Congress Cataloging in Publication Data

Ryan, William Michael.
    To die in Latin / William Ryan.
      p. cm.
    ISBN 0-89924-089-5 (cloth) : $19.95. —
ISBN 0-89924-088-7 (paper) : $9.95
    1. Political poetry, America. I. Title.
PS3568.Y397T6 1994
811'.54—dc20   94-10673
                                                    CIP

Lynx House Press
Box 640
Amherst, MA 01002

and

9305 SE Salmon Ct.
Portland, OR 97216

Lynx House Press books are distributed by Small Press Distribution, 1814 San Pablo Avenue, Berkeley, CA 94702.

Contents

From its beginning this work has been dedicated to the conspicuous absences, loss and recovery, to the transformational potential of depression and therefore to hope.

I want to thank Andy Robbins for his comments on the work and Chris Howell for his continued encouragement.

I

TIEMANN PLACE

—for Carlos Rodríquez

There comes a time, apparently, after a big mistake—
it's as natural as balding—if you have any doubt at all—
even if briefly upon waking—pieces falling in your eyes.
There comes a time, evidently, when you look into the mirror
in the bathroom, though it can be any mirror, and your face
just isn't there. Naturally you take it seriously.

You look around yourself, expecting very little really,
expecting by now the bald spot—you look around, and your home
isn't there to live in; the familiar window across the alley
with the back of the radio visible for so long—it's not there;
and your block, your neighborhood, having always been there,
with minor changes over the years—your block isn't there
to walk around; downtown isn't downtown; the city is gone;
the planet beneath your feet isn't beneath your feet.

This is a time for decisions, but there are no choices.
This is a time to consult the oracles, but there are no oracles.

There are a few things you can do at a time like this:
you can be grateful that you apologized in advance
and make another big mistake; you can try to be brave,
fat chance. If there's anything left, maybe, you can try
to form it into an outline, however sketchy, of a face.
Make it angelic if you want. Then you can begin working outward
from the mirror. You can try to build a home, doubt by doubt,
then your block, impossibly, the city next, if there's time
before you begin to worry about the planet at your feet
and its pieces.

TROUBLE IN HEAVEN

White carpets
are for the dead. The living
walk on pain, as we know,
but the dead, even here,
even the ones who died smiling,
they suffer without rest.
They make me nervous.
I'm so withdrawn in heaven
I'm like a bus. I fear
I'll never be able to talk
entirely in clichés. I think *lemon*
and someone else's mouth waters.

Sleeping is what you do
when there's nothing else to do,
like now, in heaven. I try to see
if I can fall asleep
with my eyes open. I balance my body
first, then my mind. I stop smiling
and frowning and I sleep
for a moment. Did I
miss anything? A redefinition of self?
One breath of the unconscious double?
I know there were bombs. *Someone*
was tortured for God.

I should shun the devils?
As they signal me from the perimeter?
Flashing a bottle of something
dangerous in the moonlight? Calling me forth?
I who grow weaker in heaven, thinner,
translucent, shivering under blankets?
Where is the rag-haired psychoflower
of purgatory, beating the pulse in her
neck against my mouth parted in sleep?

I could get involved
in a good science, maybe,
and not be caught dead
thinking about God,
entertain myself with six wry anecdotes
about metallurgy. Metallurgy is actually
very interesting. There's a world of color
beneath the microscope, indicating
certain things about what acid to use
to accomplish certain things.
There's an urgency
with which I make my observations
for science. Soon I'll have to burn
the holy orchard to save my life.

There are parts of heaven I like
and will miss: the Godlike vegetables
of my hands, the book from which I rise
to smell a flower, the quiet shelter
of the bed by the moon, the seemingly endless
allotment of time to prepare
a meal and eat it at a table with a proper chair
and a gesture of good will.

I leave them the times tables.
I leave them my white rat,
no longer capable of being himself.

BLUR OF EDGES

The usual smoke is rising,
the fat man walking his dog.
Maybe I half-notice how he walks
differently today,
because he's wearing gloves, perhaps—
or, more as if he were wearing fur,
had less cerebrum, more grace,
less hesitation. Maybe I half-notice
pigeons tucked into arches
of the cupola, finding a slice of light
to warm them, or how I blink back
from serious distance—I don't know
what she's saying. I nod, agreeing
to a color or a number, affirming
some notion I really can't.

The rose in the sky turns
gray, spirited away
this swiftly, draining
from the eyes. Dusk comes in
lights from unknown dimensions,
amber along the interstate
then silver and red in circles
of Hell. The cluster
of fast-food joints blooms,
headlights escaping above
the coiling of hills.

I wait for this moment
to make of me a lower
threshold, so I can tolerate
less, so I might overflow
in public, so rivulets will run
where I walk, and where I've stood
for a time, watching a child
or a dirty squirrel find its way,
puddles will form, and where I've lived
and left my emanations on things,

a river will come of the accumulation,
then a confluence of rivers,
and all at once, from source to mouth,
the reaching and final emptying
that brings the planet
to the shores of Jersey,
spirit like blood
to the flesh of cheeks,
night to itself in wonder
and a longing for opening
to some opening
in the moment we have together.

BELLS

In the dark without
paper or pencil,
without anything
remembered, he figures
five bells
represent five o'clock.
It seems perfect.
He doesn't move a muscle.
He has never read a book.
He has never tasted flesh.
He hears his mother's laugh
muted in death like jazz, whole
notes surrounded by black,
no memory of the preceding note,
no knowledge of the next, no need
to break fast. Now
the task is to figure
what five o'clock represents,
if he stirs his bones at all,
which he does not,
if he smacks his tongue for food,
which he does not,
if he remembers.
Don't let him remember.

ROOM

There's an old man coughing
in the next room.
It's a dry cough. In some ways
I'm glad you're not around to see
this view from the room,
men outside unloading dead chickens,
though if you couldn't read the sign
on the truck you wouldn't know it,
the way they're so neatly dead.
So fresh you'll taste the difference,
it says. These chickens will be eaten.
They're definitely not fresh,
you can tell from here. They're dead.
All thoughts from now on are about death.
I've learned that much.
In this way I'm religious.

This man wants to be alive more
than anything. Is that convincing?
Will you rest in peace now?
He of course would love
if he could
to play music, and why not
saxophone, phallus of the soul,
bent for fucking around corners?
He of course would love if he could
to go back home, and why not
Jersey, testing ground
of the Future Cars?
His door to the world
is gone, sure. No, he can't explain
himself.

There's no blood on the apron of the man
who unloads dead chickens. I'm waiting
by the window for the Future Cars.
I'm waiting for the bright rain.
I'm waiting for something a lot worse.

Dead chickens don't need to be eaten.
I've learned that much
In this way I'm religious.

They can just lie there
and rot, for example,
until they stop delivering
them, until barges of them
are double-parked off Long Island.
But what can save the heart?
Not the president.
The heart can give only so much,
and then it gives some more.

There's a point at which things become
serious. This is that point. The chickens
just keep coming off the truck
for a long time now. What I thought
was coughing is distant intermittent
hammering. I must have known
there's no old man
in the next room—
there's no one in the next room.

Field

*"Lawrence, already halfway out the door, thinks
I am about to be dead."*

—Adam Hammer
from "Lawrence is Funny"

So what if Jonathan Edwards is still
preaching under this New England steeple
jutting into a region of space
characterized by the physical property
of gravity—physics and religion
can get along here. Surely
this is civilization. One dead language
talks to another. The morning moon pales
in the blue laws. Pigeons line up
on the peak, fall one by one, over
the years. The sky is deep red, streaked
black and white with night and day,
but let's not make too much of it—
I suspect the world is always this strange,
and we its horrible workers.

A man dies, true, and I
have time on him, don't I? I'm not sure
he doesn't want it this way. What a joke
he makes of this beautiful sunrise
rising in the middle of a sunrise!
He gives it woolen lips or ski boots,
or miniature police cars cruising
the dark woods on big paper plates,
and sets it in Ecuador and calls it Blakean,
suggesting that men die all the time,
so to avoid the obvious we must create
black capsules of incorrigible laughter
and swallow them, until something less
like real life comes along.

After the seventh shot
whiskey becomes politically incorrect,
I understand, especially at daybreak,
but look how much room I have!
Page after page with no people
to butt in, time after time,
but I don't mean to start a god-
damned one-man therapy group
or have myself falling fragilely
through the autumnal voice of leaves
or have a genius finding in the most red
stratum of sky a skull with the brain
in tact, as if to excavate deep image
from refracted light. Physics is physics,
and the dead—now, the dead
have time on their hands,
both hands. I have one hand
attacking the other.

       Beneath the lamp Henry Miller rants
about America. Few people are awake.
The pigeons bank toward the windows,
swoop toward Main. A woman pronounces old Irish
in a slow chant at the kitchen table, arms crossed
on her breasts. I begin my daily constitutional—
the seeking of light, brilliance even, obstructed
by my nervous shirt and pants, by the clock
and the politics of the chair and table in translation,
by nuclear explosions leaping around
the edge of the sun and by dense configurations
of throbbing molecules devouring and evacuating
shamelessly, playing grab-ass in the kitchen
like poor Italians with too many kids already.

       There I am down on the corner, looking right
then wrong, waiting, depending on the way one moment
seems to lead to the next to get me by. I have no car.
Even my heels are worn, gloriously. No one arrives
to ask me if I want to live gently in the floral home
of a dead nature poet for free and take my meals
at the Poet's Commissary. I don't mind.

I don't like cars. What am I doing down there?
I look suspicious, like a criminal
with a concealed strophe. It looks like I'm drinking
from a styrofoam cup—probably coffee
with a shot of whiskey, probably good whiskey.
I'm thinking of how many times
I must have heard Dylan's *Like a Rolling Stone*—
it frightens me every time,
but I don't want to make something of it.

    We're turning off Sixteenth onto Ocean Ave
in 1966. It's Greg driving.
I have my arm out the window of the '56 Chevy,
people in swimsuits around the hot-dog stand,
the sea sailing away as far as the eye can see.
In the Top-Ten Countdown Dylan asks,
"How does it feel?" I have no idea.
But at that moment I know I will always be turning
that corner like this. It's no ecstatic vision.
It's solitary, full of dread and abstraction,
like dying in Latin. Even in youth, youth is gone,
as the body jerks clumsily in and out
of what was once graceful.

    Water is boiling. The clock looks over
my shoulder. I'm not doing anything at all.
A very sad paint job is in the kitchen.
I give up the search for light by breathing
deeply, by eating toast with tea. Autonomically
I conspire to be several heartbeats away,
the sky less red now, the kaddish of Irish intoning,
the '56 pressed into a two-foot cube somewhere.
A voice from a book in the other room says
there is faith. We both look up, the woman
in the middle of the Irish word for *the man*
is illuminated, I in the middle
of a particularly interesting doubt.
We look quizzically at each other and shrug.

    A woman in pink pants suit plays
Take Me Out to the Ball Game on accordion

on a weedy softball diamond in Birmingham—
it can only be a funeral for Adam.
He says something like his body feels
really hurt being dead. He has people laughing
because they don't believe he's really dead
this time, as he disappears into an igloo
among the kudzu. If you knew him you'd know
what I mean, though I don't mean anything.
The fact of the head-on means nothing to me
about accidents. Maybe he wants to take
some son-of-a-bitch with him. It's a risk
being around him—this is his poetry.
For a eulogy I read aloud his poem,
The Soft Outfield, which doesn't mean anything,
hearing him laugh at my seriousness.

       I'm halfway out the door.
No one arrives to slaughter me a calf
and ask me if I want to go home. I don't mind.
I don't eat veal. The toaster oven disappears.
"I hate that," the woman says. I grow a second hand
with which to hack off the hour hand
and I hack it off, take my keys off the nail.
She puts a hairbrush in her purse.
We go down the elevator, hit the street
at a good clip. She goes straight,
as she always does, and I turn the corner
with the ace of hearts marking my place
in Henry Miller. It takes one man
about a year to dismantle the universe—
I never knew that before.

PATERSON REUNION

"For twenty years I haven't been able to mention the soul."

—Juan Flores, combat vet, at the funeral of a vet suicide

Sun rising slowly to light
on the Passaic River sheen
of mercury between silk
mills long extinct
shadows
black cat in tenement window
saxophone in morning
prayers, white cat in lower window
washing his feet behind frosted glass
curtain breathing in and out, cathedral bells
deep grumbling of something unearthed
garbage truck gears uphill at this defenseless
hour of mourning, but this may be expected—
it's almost a natural sound, the way silence
is decomposed by a waterfall
and reassembled downriver.

"Twenty years," Juan says, in passing
in this passing, in this *que paso*
we are as strange as we are familiar
over coffee, eggs with *platanos* on red plates,
guavas blended with sugar and water,
faces limp as brilliant flags passing
in the heat, fruit colors of the market behind.

Since it became known that white skin
was the result of the great loss
of pigment, not the vestments
of redemption, and recessive genes dominated
the erotic infinite—since some spooky short-timer
from the 1st Cav took a bite of a VC liver and left
it there to speak for the damned, he hasn't been able
to mention the soul, not as it relates to Cuban
heels, not as it appears in the Poetry

of Books, not in the form of the Holy
Ghost, not in record stores in the *barrios*
of Paterson. This morning he says it—
soul. Not because he feels any better, not because
he heard neighborhood poets or Hilton Ruiz
jam with Paquito D'Rivera or because of the seriousness
of playground basketball, not because the woman
with the gold tooth or the earth
with all its miraculous medals moved
beneath him this morning, the hard-working
Passaic shining seaward, but because it's so simple
in this Jersey accent, among those who have endured
by mutually agreeing to endure.

A teenage boy joins us, tells us he's staying
with his hard-luck sister in a room
big enough for a bed and a few dozen stuffed animals
until his parents, back from failing
to make a new start in Maine, find jobs
and a place to live. He wants to be with someone
because his sister is at work
and her boyfriend, just out of jail, is already gone.

We deny him twice, put off
by his intrusion. A man comes in
with a carburetor, a vee of geese passes
in juke box salsa. We ask the boy
if he wants to walk. We walk. He talks
of his peptic ulcers, daily injections
and how he took a lighter to his shirt
and jumped down the hole of a stairwell.

The day is still
as fresh as a flapping fish, fireman
shooting hoops, a brother in a beat
Camaro, singing with the radio.

On the greened copper flashing
bent over the peak of the church, a pigeon
has mounted another pigeon and floats
above her, flapping, standing on her light
as a feather, but she flies away.

"Fly!" Juan yells—"fly away!"
The boy looks at him oddly.
The flag is flying over everything.
A fat woman eats a doughnut in her car.

We go back to the church to light a candle
for what defects from the isolation
of the body for the isolation of the soul.

"THE SOLO YOU TOOK ON A SOLO OF MINE"

—for Steve Lacy

If you consider the soprano
saxophone in solo, abandoning scales
for higher and lower scales,
tearing down the margins of error,
or easing the distance between two points,
or coloring the walls an easier color,
or drawing smoke from the rectory chimney
as snow falls, notated for baritone,
or as a half-slip lies wilted on the floor,
or as headlights leave their rank and file,
silent above the distant highway,
and not a word.

If you consider singularity,
presented as such—a man flying,
or an old woman helping an old woman,
or an anxious stand of cypresses,
or fish guts staining the fisherman's pants,
or anything with beautiful lines—
a woman in a nightgown pouring tea,
the clutter of her hair, this promise,
and not a word.

If you consider how high in joy
the feet can be lifted off the ground,
and how frequently renewable,
a certain curve made by the back and leg,
skip step inserted in the walk,
playful antics of the left arm,
gesticulated offering of the heart,
white space arranging it all
among the drum beats,
and not a word.

If you consider the turning of the body
in its three dimensions, small explosions

against its boundaries, vast implosions
against the spirit, the ever changing face,
eyes coming out to touch eyes, bones connected
in beauty, the tidal flooding in the groin,
and not a word.

If you consider the shudder of glory
recorded in the alcohol-level of blood,
the moment of geese and moon alignment,
the slip of land between God and shark,
angles of rooftops baffling city planners
with metaphysics, the ways of disappearance
multiplying outward toward the seasons,
the pupa, the gibbous, the green of the apple,
and in the tall grass two holes
through which the world sees itself,
and not a word.

If you consider how the void would regenerate
around the void, how the wound in time would heal,
how one hand can't hack off the hand,
how two hands are necessary to hack off the hand—
if you consider this, I might sing along,
I might celebrate a holiday,
I might bomb Cambodia,
and not a word.

If the suburb would erupt, maybe—
if the dead walked as a point of illustration
I might agree,
I might consult imaginary people in high positions
when everyone else has gone to sleep,
the signals all blinking amber,
a 'possum with two red lights leading the way.

I turn to look out the window as a tree falls—
over the curve of its spirit
is strewn a diaspora of ants.

CRUX

Thirty thousand feet below, humankind
is human for all of us, the way we are human

for each other, human where others are not.
Look at our shadow—this is from where

the crucifix came, flying and folding over
our dwellings like its back ain't got no bone—

the cross of the crossed and double-crossed.
The woman in slippers, limping, isn't limping,

graciously, to manipulate the heartstrings.
She doesn't want to go to the shelter anyway.

Certainly the boy isn't down there,
not sleeping on newspaper beside his father.

The man with no money really has money,
hidden in his illusive number of days.

The crazy one with the shopping cart....
Look how many coats he has, and there's a sandwich

now, falling from his garbage bag.
The food they aren't hungry for isn't there,

fortunately, to complicate things.
For the professor beside me, theoretically,

no distinctions are made between things.
That's what she said. It must be interesting

the way no distinctions are made between things.
For the man behind the curtain with cocktail,

"This is a classless society," and I bet it
does look that way from his house,

the way from up here we all seem to be intelligible
engineers of order with places to go and places to live.

PLANETARY

Marsh grass lacquered in clear
ice picks up two lights:

sunside, two blue herons,
heads above the grass;

white steeple to the moonside
behind the tree line.

A goose spiralling, wings blown
back then tumbling, all black

and white, head over tail,
flailing on the loose neck.

NO HELP

I meant to ask the shepherd, Miguel
the real name and etymology of *cervix*.

I'm supposed to agree that he shouldn't
be birthing its lambs without knowing

labia majora and *minora*, for example.
I'm supposed to consider, in Latin,

the disenfranchised abstract meat employees,
working on the final solution

to what it will eat. I'm supposed to accept
that because it kills it will have to gnaw itself

from this life to another, that the oracles
fall short of this always, that back to nature

is not far enough back, that the six senses
are no help, that the seventh would make

no difference, that there is no help.
Nevertheless, I'm supposed to look around

for help. I'm supposed to understand that alcohol,
for example, might make it clear

one way and sobriety another, and I'm not supposed
to be influenced by either. I'm not supposed

to notice that the fact that it doesn't exist
doesn't stop it.

I'm supposed to believe
God was born of this.

WHERE TO BEGIN

You observe from a distance the sea
at the brink of suburbia—
and in the sky, escaped headlights,
three bright points on a vertical plane.

You observe by moonlight the times tables,
spinning in a very simple cosmology,
which you understand almost completely.

You observe phosphorescent organisms,
each of their feet in a cell
of salt water, pitching forward lyrically
every seven seconds with the rotation
of a low-impact microwave antenna.

Your head grows a foot sadder,
like a glacier and a sea mammal,
too fraught to levitate with hope,
too far gone for trick language.

And from your soul, which, you observe,
has the wingspan of a housefly,
comes an image: cherubic little twits
holding up electric lights, benign mathematics
tangled in the borderwork,

and in the detail, two words
sadder than one, three words
that misrepresent the world,
no word that is not another
mistake, word nailed on top of word.

To dissect the wrist to learn more
about the hand—this isn't funny.
To call the heart *heart* and the brain
brain isn't funny. To cleave light
into color isn't funny,
revealing the lack of simplicity
prismed in a drop of dew.

Or to begin
again, stubbornly,
with the whole body,
including all the apocryphal
translucent parts and all the thoughts
in the heart and in the body
(which is a larger heart, beating openly,
brave and vulnerable) and remain nothing,
with small bravery, and something,
after all, with more bravery—
this isn't funny.

And how would you know when to stop
laughing? At the human
clapper of the bell, the upside down
smile of the face? At the club's joke
to the bone? At the killing jokes?
At the history of killing jokes?
At the man who wandered dumb
into the animal, poor thing?

And then
where to begin
again? On cue?
During the commercial?
At the brink
of suburbia? At the passing
of the first clear water?
At the third sex
of torture, Latin roots emerging
all over the mouth?

And what is
the third sex of torture
like? Like the prisoner
holding up the broken bottoms of his feet
for the third clubbing
as the torturer gets an erection?
Funny stuff.
Latin roots might be like
the foamy blood that emerged

as he said his Hail Marys,
Medivac hovering humorously
above the fires like the *what?*
The angel of death?

You could keep it to yourself.
You could be more or less sophisticated.
You could use something more textural
or something that evokes the scent evacuating
or the stickiness of the hennaed ivory—
something with *henna* anyway.

You could wade unceremoniously off the brink
of suburbia, thinking: I could lay me down
my speculations; I could receive the nest
and the axe like any tree; I could ruminate
only physically, bending with the dusk
and without pity, with darkening resolve
and without hesitation, with affirmation
in sorrow, to close
the flesh of the carnation
so the seeds may be preserved
in rags in the dura matre
and the dirt properly fecundated forward.

It becomes daybreak with fog
and description, with mistakes multiplied,
the sea itself a mistake of description,
the crab marooned in the island of the crab,
fish images broken off
from exotic accretions of alluvium—
and a man, pants crotch almost to his knees,
Greek fisherman's cap, mistaking in every direction,
but kind of funny, like a cockroach circumventing
a foot.

He makes you want to say *funny*
over and over until it sounds funny.
He makes you want to do funny things in public.
He makes you want to allow *something* to be funny
and trust that *it is* funny, beyond the mortal
and irreligious tomb.

II

TROPISM IN RELIGIOUS PAINTING IN THE PRADO

Sacrificer of box turtles,
supple as apple boughs,
sexual as the milkweed pod,
radiant and dancing trancelike at catechism,
a frail boundary of light holding you,
bound only by the weight of the earth,
the turtle your totem among the numens,
you're a child stabbing yourself,
wounding yourself in the child God
in the trees in the background.

Charged with utter simplicity, you touch
the tart green then sweet ripe fruit
falling to fermentation of apples—
seasons turn this gently in your fingers.
You're a deer in the aim of an arrow.
Flecks of sun depart daily and don't return,
on the osprey's flight, on the ground hog
swallowed by the hole, on sheets drying
in late afternoon. Clear water pours
from your fright, your eyes averting each other
under kitchen neon. Something dead
is put in your mouth, something warm
pulled over your fear. The first
times table is administered.

You're the driver of the Future Car,
sexual as newly frozen steel. You're
the man who unloads dead chickens, the man
who kills dead chickens, who births dead chickens.
The greatest sadness is in this world. This world
prepares you for anything. There is no greater pain
than in this world. Once you've lived in this world
you can live anywhere.

You pass crystals among the plague of homeless,
benevolent as snow on a steeple.

You're a padre bathing his ocher bones
on the third floor of the rectory
in the fifty-seventh year of his life,
naked in his skeleton
in the old tub with turtle's claws
with his opportunity to be ashamed or not.
One Hail Mary could open the flood gates now.

You're more like the trees in the background,
less like the cock with its comb,
strutting ostentatiously about the nether mouth.
You won't be seduced by her.

The nether mouth is simply the nether mouth.
She has long been thought of as death,
and is at last just that.
(Now what will you do,
the cock in your killer's hands?)

You could call her many things
but know better. You make the black offering
of fish eggs—you're not cheap about it.
She likes exotic imported fish eggs,
sticking like fish eggs to their lovely gum,
fish eggs you could call many things
but know better. Fish eggs are as much like
fish eggs as anything, so you offer them
as they are, on a silver platter,
in the foreground, but you won't be seduced.

Your dance of the bitch in heat is too lewd
and too funny. Looking into her eyes with mirrors,
you don't know what to do—
you draw something on the ground with flour—
you don't know what—it tends toward a circle—
it becomes a housefly—you erase it,
pretending you're supposed to.

You have Laszlo Toth's hammer, the Virgin Basher.
Why? Well, figuring *what the hell*—
he got out in three years,

and *he* thought *he* was Jesus—
shattered her left arm, broke her nose, left
eye and veil. Fifty fragments
were recovered for the reconstruction.
If it wasn't for the Italian fanatic
who pulled him down, Toth would have had her all,
so you raise it, nail the human form
up against its glorification, beat to death
your very important point.

You're like the trees, limbs outstretched,
gesturing stupidly to the suburb,
not like the rooster scratching at her feet.
How could you be seduced?

The blossoms, having already fallen, lyrically—
well, you decide, wisely, to leave it
to the *cante jondo*, for example,
to have the damned things resurrect themselves
on the banks of El Cuerpo Del Hombre, for example.
You decide to leave it to the Italian fanatic
kneeling with the O in his mouth
before the purely representational dark background
of wilderness, her wilderness,
the bullets of sweat barely visible now in the trees.

You prefer to let them remain dead blossoms,
neither resurrecting nor nurturing
even your very important point.
In this way you owe her nothing—
no debt to the angels or the poets.
Sexually, you resemble a tree.
You feel about her the way a tree might feel
about its dirt. In this way
she can't seduce you, surely
not while you're sleeping beside the lamb.

You won't be seduced by the folkie names
of regional plantlife overtaking the *plaza mayor*
or by the unembellished weed olive in flat
midday sun. Her dicotyledonous urge to spread
and send forth leaves can't seduce you,

though it brought you feelings of secular humanism,
though suddenly you wanted to be seduced,
there and then, carried away immobilized like Toth,
his face cast in the look of Florentine awe,
befitting of a man whose folklore hates the earth.
You're a tree, draped in vestments of dark background.

The woman she sent from the swimsuit issue or
the three pretty girls in their ultraviolet underwear
can't seduce you. The apostles or sub-apostles
or the neo-apostolic verse thrown up in holiness
can't raise your sap, can't undercut your seriousness
with seriousness, can't save your awful humor
from its own funny demise. Still, you love her
singing, especially the way it is of this earth,
a singing with a physical responsibility
to the physical. You love it sloppy, hazardous,
audible then not. You don't love it because
of its fleeting nature—you love it when it stops
only so the even less profound can be heard.
But you won't be seduced by this song you love.
You're like a tree in the background.

The weed olives stoop, make themselves scarce—
they want nothing to do with you.
They pretend they don't know you.
They're a thousand years old,
and they'd like to keep it that way.

The full moon is whatever you need it to be
in this unseasonable heat, at the risk of lyricism
and despite its autumnal weariness with harvests,
tidal business and courtships—it's seen diffused
then unseen in the steam, creaking on the slackwater,
apparently astray from more tropical moods.

It raises up your stem a dark liquid and leaves open
a taste crystallized on the back of your tongue,
beyond where the tongue tastes the deliciousness
of the third deadly sin, which is, of course, Lust,
where it mingles with Love on the back of your tongue.

The groves green a bit more, a surge
in the spent tomato plants, crickets revived
in their jive doxologies, female spoor at large
in the *campo* among the various cautions, darker skin
stretched over older bones for a deeper drum.
Sixteen-year-olds push forth with this rhythm
into childbirth, cervixes dilated
into the circle of the family.

Bacteria and viruses flourish in this heat—
disregard this. The water is not potable,
but disregard that. A teaspoon of dirt
goes into every dish, two in the chicken with rice.
Cicadas are too big to appear in poems,
so disregard them. You can watch a cockroach
climb Piety Street Tavern from across the street,
at night, without your glasses, half drunk,
the other half about to really make it.

You smell the sugared almonds of Andalucía;
you know enough to poach an egg in the garlic soup;
you have no scruples about the roast suckling pig;
the *rioja* pools along your lower lip,
soaking the end of the cigarette you keep burning
as you eat. You have little choice but to breathe
the unfamiliar aroma of her hair then inhale deeply
along the strands of confinement then fall over drunk
in her innermost recess—no, in her *seno*—
the Spanish is better. You don't know what it is
in English, but certainly not *innermost recess.*

But it's too humid to be Andalucía—you wonder
what language is spoken in Djakarta and if
there is a word like *seno* among Indonesian dialects—
or, better, a deeper word, and you wonder if Java
is even tropical enough, as your entire body curls
upward like cigarette smoke around a trumpet vine.

Just before sleep you know she's coming
by what precedes her: sublime resignation, authentic

poetic lines, serious doubts leaving like bats
from the soul, mnemonics designed to remember her
essential appendages and their very important points,
the spilling of seeds from a cracked melon,
the sticky sweet minerals of her bath, sex falling
off her so vividly you can crystallize it
and fold it in paper for later, a blossom
and two bullets whining out of the dark background.

Just as you slip beneath her the bullets enter—
it's difficult to remember the details
with two bullets in the head—high velocity, .22 magnum,
very professional, cloudy sources, vaguely authorized
three-piece suits intimidating the prosecution.
Maybe they were God's bullets. Can God have bullets,
after Franco, never mind use them, in sequence,
as if one moment is followed by another,
one spinning around inside the skull, remarkably,
like at the rollerderby, lodging above the ear,
and the other somehow causing a limp?

She takes your head in her oiled hands and soothes it
to a halt, but for all its unpredictable turns,
you know it would be better off
barreling in the unguarded orbits
than propped in these tuberous fingers
illuminated dimly like ampules of milk.
You know nothing reasonable of the language
beyond her, and she swaddles you in laurel
for this lack of knowledge,
the drowsy infant unborn
and opening outward from inside you.
You're ready to keep unlearning.
There is no greater pleasure than the pleasure of this world.
In this world you are no one.
This world prepares you for nothing.
This world spoils you for others.

III

GIVE IT UP

I give up
cigarettes. It takes eight years
of weaning, but I give it up.
I give up drugs in spite
of Nancy Reagan. I just say no.
I give up alcohol, one day at a time,
though it's a cherished heirloom.
I give up Haagen Dazs—too much fat.
I give it up. I give up coffee.
It brings me down
after it brings me up,
so I give it up. I give up salt.
After ten thousand millennia my cells
lose their taste for salt. I give it up.
I give up meat. Not just red meat.
Meat is dead animals. I no longer know
why I would want to put dead animals
in my mouth. I give it up. I give up
leather shoes and leather belts
and leather underwear and really sad
articles about how animals suffer
for taste. I give up fur and fur underwear.
I give up everything that profits off destruction
of the rain forest—McDonald's and beef dog food,
mahogany and rosewood furniture,
chopsticks and Mitsubishi. I give up everything
that's tested on animals—lipstick and eyeliner
and hair spray. I give up South African diamonds.
I just say no to diamonds.
I give up hot dogs.
Hot dogs lead to baseball,
and baseball is a frivolous escape,
like a drug. I give it up.
I give up women. Women can be a drug.
It feels good, there's a dependency,
a rush, a crash, and women are too smart.
I give up masturbation. It was fun
for a while, but masturbation is narcissistic.

I need to get out of myself, but not that way.
I give it up. I give up the pursuit of happiness
and of heaven and settle for an extended stay
in purgatory. I give up the pursuit of comfort
and settle for the absence of excruciating pain.
Comfort is a drug. It kills the soul.
I give it up. I give up the pursuit of money
and go back to teaching. Money doesn't buy happiness.
Anyway I've already given up happiness.
I give up what money does buy—
tolerance. I give it up.
I give up writing. Writing can be an excuse
for failing at everything, including writing.
Writing can be a habit. It leads to heavier stuff,
like thinking. I give up thinking. I just meditate,
and when I have a thought, I think,
Get thee behind me thought, and I think,
a hot dog and a late-night Lana Turner movie
would be nice, and I give it up. I give up TV.
TV is a drug. It leads to violence
by simulating activity and blurring the line
between imagination and reality.
I give up imagination in favor of reality.
I give up laughing and crying in favor of understanding.
I try to understand.
I try to understand.
I give it up.
What's left?
It's Saturday night.
I got some money 'cause I just got paid.
I stand in the kitchen. What are my options?
Walk to the living room and stand there.
A.A. meeting. Knit for the hospice.
Rent a dirty movie, put on a Tammy Wynette record
and Hoover for a while, do my ironing
strutting around in front of the mirror,
talking dirty to myself in my sheerest slip,
the one with blood stains,
and batter myself, get the iron real hot...
What's left?
Death. I give up death.

I just say fuck it.
I give it up. What's left?
Life. Ah, life—something I can't give up.
I get hungry.
Maybe some chocolate and a chili dog.
I feel like dancing.
Dance steps like footprint diagrams
connected by arrows emerge
from the pattern of my genetic code.
There's a tricky couple of steps
over and under the double-helix of my DNA.
Other people who resemble my aunts and uncles
and sisters and cousins and mom and dad
are dancing in the background.
Behind them are two holes
through which the world sees itself,
and behind that—could it be?
I can almost make out something
bigger than all of us,
something too big to see,
something pretty amazing in spite of itself,
something I'll never understand,
so I laugh, then I cry,
then I manage a small feeling of wonder
and a particularly interesting doubt.

LACUNAE

After death the sea is calm
as a loading dock when idling trucks depart
and traffic static is almost soothing, aqueous,
washing the indefinite edge. The body
gets its legs under it, stands,
goes looking for food in a strange town,
a four-car funeral passing through the red light.

Given our nature to shelter
in rags or caves or suburbs
or varying degrees of sleep
or love, given the choice between perfection
of the life or of the art,
it's even more difficult
to imagine a new life
than it is to imagine this one,
the plaster cracked with a certain light
that goes easy with gitano violins
and makes much of the particularly
Iberian cob webs above the hams,
a subtle wrenching in the metaphysical
realm of the chest, requiring death
to be more than we might want
it to be, and this making it all
worth it.

Our sweaters, which we set afloat
on the outgoing tide, are knitted
with patterned stitches that identify us
as those who won't return from so far
into the north country they don't understand
our sandals or our tans. We want simply
to walk among them in the hardware store
without them saying, "There goes
What's-Their-Names and their efforts
to be like us, with chinos
and crow's feet around the eyes,"
but we must order our eggs with tell-tale

gentleness, for they are too curious
with their plates of brownies
and their helping hands.

Not a soul will bother to forget us
here, excellent hashish infusing the orange trees,
and above the gypsy caves in its rhinestone collar
a ceramic dog rests as it did in life,
the moment paralyzed in longing for itself
but affirming everything, including the amber light
in the lead-glass window over the oaken portal
we pause before, as if this could satisfy us.

We locate a remote chair and table
in a paler light more sympathetic
to the diminution of light
and we sit, sweep this light
with a soft brush, spread a cloth
and uncork some generous spirit,
preparing for an uneventfulness
we might as well count
among our blessings.

We continue to fumble
with our change, delete and add
keys to our chain, locking and unlocking
our downward adjustments, coming and going
like half-familiar jazz phrases
we remember passing each day
on our returns to what we once
again think will be okay.
We watch people sail into adventures
and return as anachronisms
of themselves with moustaches
or without moustaches, having given up
all hope of harboring
mysterious agonies.

We peruse old photos,
searching for an era
when our faces were different

from the way we imagine them
on the barren lawn
that we would dig and rake
and plant by hand
after we moved down from the city
for the sake of the kids.
yet to be conceived
and never to be born.

       Maybe if we were younger
we'd stand a chance of being
more than photorealism,
or if the midget at the fruit stand
wasn't unavoidably artistic
in our eyes, or if the old church
wasn't a cosmology museum,
or our hellos weren't fraught
with an overworked plainness,
or if somehow we were able
to take a child
in each hand
to cross the street.

       We've wound up buried
in a city we would never have guessed,
borrowing jumper cables from the couple
in the trailer next door,
far from the graves of the family
and forgotten like the stories,
like the one where great-uncle Jack,
while visiting Granpop at the firehouse,
woke in the dark to use the head
and fell down the hole
to his death.
Who remembers that?

WE NOTE THE PASSING OF THE AUTHOR OF *FREUD THE ANGEL*

I. Notebook Among the Personal Effects

Your catacombed diagrams
of the missing heart are more interesting
than a lot of the stuff around.
One is like an overripe tomato
hanging in the dark, another
like a crippled person on a bus,
another like two hands parting
for their own good. We see,
among the useful chambers,
places that have no use at all.
It's this uselessness you annotate
at length. You ask us to consider
the place that ruins a person's life
with goodness—what good is it?
You're right—it should be cut out
or disconnected. There should be
some procedure for this.

You indicate the hairy deity
beneath the holy pool, suggesting
that it might be different
if we could bucket out the pool,
ride on his shoulders into the forest,
have a meal with him and be calm about it,
never wishing we were somewhere else
or feeling the urge to kill him
to save the soul, which we can't begin
to diagram without admitting too much
about what we don't know.

In the elaborate fortress, you indicate
walls of solid ruby, walls of fire.
You note the ornamental designs
on the wall of lead, intricate roses
made of sand. There is no one

singing like a fool atop the spire,
and I like that. I don't see anything
wrong with this. I would say
you are poor and honest. I would say
that if you want to wear a coat
in ninety-degree heat, that's up to you.
I would say you can sit where you want,
for as long as you want—
here's a coffee and a day-old bagel.

       You could have awakened us too early,
reciting terrible ironies below our windows
on the one morning we can sleep.
You could have taken out your eyes with a spoon
or found a crown or a cape or a baby carriage
to occupy you the way a prayer flag
occupies the wind. Instead you thought
something was missing from somewhere
and it might be a heart. I don't know
what's so wrong with this.

II. *Obiter Dictum*

Studying oil in vinegar, smoke in air,
he had successfully suspended the thought
in brine and bombarded it
with what he'd managed to contain
of what saturated the solution
when he kicked out the bottom
of infancy one night in the park.
He had demanded then
of his body a weightlessness
of flame leaping
until his spine grew
grotesque with counterbalances
to stay alive.

It was by the frequency of tambourines
replacing the moons among his papers,
the experimental ease
with which the right foot was left
forward, the garlic stink
of his bed sheets in the hovel
under the stairs that we see
he was an artist, and this explains it,
with a book and a card table
and a satchel of necessities upsetting
the slumberous turning of our stomachs.

The mothers shoulder baskets
in three languages to the fire,
many hands of carnations
washed with soap of the supposed
fat of angels, stained with rose water
and glycerin. A milky light blows ashore,
its cloth worn thin between them
with the slept-in smell of animal,
between the mothers and him,
and this explains it, with a shirt
diminished inappropriately beyond
his knowledge, embarrassing
in his close quarters
the public spectacle.

He had been tricked by love
into the threshold of physical brilliance
like a plum tearing with all its weight
from the stem. The transformation
to discourse of the spittle methodically
hidden clearly in a glass of water by his bed
was witnessed one Sunday by workers
at chessboards in the Square,
and this explains it, with a distended
unsightliness disadvantaged
horribly among the well-intended.

The fathers turn from the ruptured boat
he painted. He had recorded signatures
of crabs, trying to warn us
of what we secretly knew.
He had slept in unwashed skins there,
wet from the moon, seeing luminescent circles
when his eyes closed from steering so long
toward the fluke print of the soul.
He had stood plainly, falling invisibly
from his ivory bones like meat he lifted
in parable from seasoned rice.
He had crafted gifts with tools
of his griefs, tools dug from below
the family graves, tools that work
a smooth sadness into strong women,
and with these tools he had opened
his chest as a precondition to evidence.
Drums begin, gulls circling, bells, a mirage
gathering into colors, a few last words sparking
before they disappear beyond warehouses,
and this explains it, with fat and frankincense,
gluey flour and hearts about to explode
in the carefully balanced hunger.

III. Autopsy: A Seeing For Oneself

The body is seventy percent water,
twenty percent dirt, ten percent other,
touched by a fierce giving, itself a gift
in the already luxurious grace.
It smells like dirt, can be formed into dolls
like mud. How it cared within its community
of urges for the way the heart
was intimately involved
with the brain, the wrists
intricately connected to the hands,
for the way, in its small kitchens,
it made ends meet. Even the chickens
kept in the scrappy lots of kindness
scratched among tangible mysteries.
There is a membrane in the innermost ear
to shimmy with the kind of samba that goes on
in the lobe for the blurting out of uncontrolled
sentences. There are sounding gourds
to mellow the timbre of notes bent
to the magnetic loops of the poles.
In striations of the small of the back,
records of extinct weeds, idle thumbs,
dances with which things were named.
Fish broke water in the iris, circles
radiated out creeks that run to the plains.
Rain fell in countable drops in the dirt.

TROPHIES

—for Annie

The moose leads a private life
of meadows, pruning, maintaining,
simplifying, providing with its back
solid ground for small birds.
It reads thick novels set in northern winters.
When the moose fell it fell on its heart,
and they couldn't roll it off its heart,
not with their Farm Boyz
or with their green mules
or with their tanks.
Its antlers didn't fit
through the humiliated door of the boxcar.
They had to reinforce the wall
just to hang its head.

The antelope is a gift
of expanse, the way emptiness gives
substance of itself. Its grace
depends on long slopes. When it fell
it fell into distance between them.
They almost lost the antelope's body
in open air, amid the nothing to hide it.
They had to double-lock the doors
against its absence.

The mountain goat is a rangy comrade,
a perfect shortstop, a tinker
that can fix your blender or your tractor.
Its heart beat after an hour of boiling.
When they hung the mountain goat
they shut the windows to stop
its beard from waving, and after
the breeze itself was forbidden,
its beard tossed in unison
with the wheat
until they cut it off.

The llama is a beast of burden
with the burden of beauty.
It picks a ship of coffee
to plant an inch of beans.
When it fell it was replaced.
Its body was appropriated from its head,
its head exiled among the murals of its dead.
It couldn't be seen upon the wall.
Though they built a frame around it,
tourists never see it.

You'd think the buffalo would have died
enough times, in its small pox blankets,
in its hanging-trees, in its price-per-pound.
The buffalo is beaten down,
and when that doesn't work it's raised up,
then beaten down
perhaps more humanely.
It was remembered in mass and forgotten
in spirit.

The jaguar takes from the moon its vision
and lends to the moon its stealth.
Its blood left perfect circles on the tile floor.
The shadow we call *the other* knows the jaguar
is its ghost. They buried its heart in lead
and erected buildings against its curse.
Still the jaguar lurks in the dense growth
beneath them.

The big horn sheep drifts
up in the wind. It seems aloof
until you get to know it.
It can live on nothing
because it has a higher calling.
They kept the big horn alive
to pump its own blood
out the catheterized vein,
but it stopped its heart
while hanging upside down
and bounded into the crevasse.

The rabbit is a vital organ,
common everywhere. It loves to feel
sunshine and rest in the precious
little time to rest. Like the golden sphere
atop a Buddhist temple, it sees everything
but itself. It sees its ova overrun
with rats. Its small heart
slipped through their fingers and was lost
among the paving stones.
The rabbit hung on the wall like an apple,
like a weed in a field of weeds.

The vulture performs the sky burials.
It gets a bad rap. Think of it
not as listless but so relaxed.
Its patience outlasts the breath,
never killing, never going hungry.
It can nap through an earthquake,
lunch through a bloodbath.
They didn't hunt the vulture—it flew in,
made itself comfortable, waited.

GRACE

—for Michael Z

A blind man waiting for the bus
complained about sports commentary
these days—"Can't tell *what's*
going on." He was standing out there
on the curb in the sounds of potential
disasters, farther than us, closer,
I think, to this grace
that let us board
and be on our way.

A man on the bus whose friend
had died—this is not an average man
sheltered in a car—he said, "My friend
has died—my friend." He said it again
to people he doesn't know, graciously
afforded ignorance, I hope,
of the ten thousand deaths outside
the windows. The color and shape
of a cow's heart, in cross-section,
by DiVinci, opened up behind us
in a colored grotto in the clouds
and evening set considerately
on us, shifting its enormity
so as not to injure us mortally.

Two pigeons cocked at the louvers
of a belfry, lurid in the grays
of living, Bob Marley bleeding
from a Walkman, the blind man
working his jaw, and the serious business
out there in the white electrical noise—
someone, you can bet, was being charged
with something. But cool air blew in
and human kindness flowed out all over
and wanted to heal everything right there
in out of the light rain.

I was thinking, if a person could
have that power, just say for instance,
someone on the bus here even,
for example, all presumptions aside
for a moment, how would he go about applying?
Would he have to earn it
with his life—I mean,
would it be that hard?
What would it take to be worthy?

I made it to the poetry group
but I had nothing to say. I watched a spider
on the screen door as I tried to get some air.
The spider was praying, I thought,
that it wouldn't have to kill again.
A woman read a poem about her husband's death.
I had nothing to say about it. I said
it's good, and it is. The world can change
in an afternoon, or in a moment
we can forget.

PRAYER FOR THE DEAD

When the dead begins
the drawing of clear water
in the peace, tell me to drink
and let go my hand. Leave me.
Mystery leaves the eulogy;
shadow leaves the bird.

When the lawn mowers stop
and I lay me down in the yard,
in the peace, the Syrian neighbors
picking figs among the goats,
tell me to eat
and let go my hand. Leave me.
Children learn to play without us;
leaves half-cover the ground already.

When the juke box stops
and the head is thrown nightward
at closing time, in the peace,
uttering the sound the new erect primate
uttered suffering the first intellection,
already longing for its superstitions,
tell me the thoughtful heart constructs
with whatever it can find—bits of red
plastic, hair—an awkward coupling
of wings and let go my hand, tell me
there is a meeting in the middle of the air
if these wings should fail me
and let go my hand. Leave me.
Mammalian heat is lost in flight,
icons banished downriver,
symbologies poured in the dirt.

When the traffic static ebbs
and the glass with my lip print stands empty
of clear water, in the peace,
when the starling lights on the weed maple
in a coming together and the fly circles,

when I'm strengthened by this example
of my own ingenious heart, and this longing
is all, except the shade scraping the sill
in the peace, tell me the radiant infant
is lowered on umbilical vine,
opens its two senses of innocence
and sees for the dead on the slab
and let go my hand. Leave me.
I become, by the Seven Mysterious Agonies,
my father, my child and my mother
when she was thirty-five and sexy,
rocking me in the second-story timbers,
the way the soul will not leave the body.

When the rainbow trout swallows the hook,
comes flashing out of the sunspot
in the fracturing of the world
and nearby a cow is standing in the rain
in the peace, tell me the face that,
when I am the luckiest of men, comes to rest
on my shoulder before its next astonishment,
is as renewable as the trees
and let go my hand. Leave me.
There is a union that precedes the union
of sperm and ovum; man and woman
with their hearts pull themselves
into one another and with their spirits
praise their spirits.

When the bank clock threatens
the pigeons and the lynx and the rabbit
twitch their noses in the forest, tell me
the teeth retract from the brain, then
from the holes they punched in the skull.
Tell me the eyes of that skull fill again
with something that appears to be light
and the two animals return to a better place
in the forest, in the peace,
and let go my hand. Tell me the old man
straightens from his task of walking,
breathes, reaches a quarter from his pocket,

bounces it and catches it on the rebound,
his hands limber and his smile
becoming boyish as his mother appears
beside him, and let go my hand.
Leave me. The boy is lifted to her bosom
and soon after drawn into her
without a whimper as her mother appears
to grow younger in the peace; one thread,
twisted of two threads, becomes untwisted
and unwoven from one intersection
of warp and woof; the bank clock
fumbles like an idiot with its dots.

NOT TO MAKE EMPTINESS A POINT OF VIEW

A small grace from the open window
tosses the blank page away,
and what's left seems more significant.
I should think of Li Po
floating his poems downriver,
waking from his nap to wonder
how many blossoms had fallen.

The rent is overdue again.
Combine crews, up from west Texas,
have moved north again, leaving O'Sullivan
passed out in the can, his pants down
around his ankles. Pappy McShane died,
leaving his fountain-pen collection
to no one. Miguel, who doesn't speak English,
is worrying in the broken metal
rocker on the porch, the bass line
of *Whiskey River* throbbing in the light
dust from the open door of The Duke.
It's all very prosaic.
Naomi added a St. Bernard pup to the four kids
in her trailer, and no one can understand why.
All these mysteries, a pot of green chili
and a blank page.

I ladle some chili to a plate,
fold a tortilla, kick the screen door open
and hunker down in the hundred degrees,
in the eighteen-inch shadow of the eaves.
My fingers have been burning since yesterday
from chopping the jalepeños. No one
can eat the chili, not even Miguel,
who's hungry. Reluctantly, I cut it in half
with pintos and onions, and still
no one can get it down.

In front of the foothills
where they bend west below Cheyenne—
grain elevator, railroad stanchion,
boarded-up storefronts, lit Coors sign
and an image: magpie in cottonwood.

How the bird is part blue,
like a piece of the Colorado sky—
how the tree is much like other trees.
I should think of Po Chü-i
destroying his five vital organs,
according to Bashö, and of Bashö
becoming absurd ahead of his time
on rice wine, anticipating the efficiency
of the Hatsukari Limited Express.

Ancient China was lush.
A drop of dew could lie for months,
waiting patiently to be observed
closely and from afar
by an antisocial oversensitive drunk
somehow capable of seeing in it
a curved replica of the world
towering to peaks above
his famous grass hat.

I retrieve the blank page
from where it's stuck on nothing apparent—
on the heat of the day rising off Route 1.

A drop falls out of the blue,
evaporates before it hits,
as it sometimes will in August.

C & W

He says, "Lemme
have some blues,"
and she gives him some.
It's a scene
you wouldn't forget. The sax man
disappears. Everybody falls
in love and begins
to ruin their lives
before the solo. Then
everything is upside down then
right side up and fake
snow is falling
on the cocktail tables. Violet
laughs without making any noise,
her shoulders jerking. Eddie
lights a Camel, looking out
at what's too big to see.
Someone on the dance floor calls Thomas
a crazy son-of-a-bitch. It's Lucy.
She and Chuck are dancing with bourbon and cokes.
In a few different places
promises are being made.
No one believes them,
except the suckers,
who are stacked up three-deep at the bar.

WILD ROSES

—for Flynn

He broke a glass today.
Now he has only one.

One will be enough.
He has a view of death.

Sometimes he smells it all around him.
Sometimes he can't smell it

because it's all around him.
Sometimes it makes him dance privately.

Sometimes he dies privately.
The books are old, books he's had too long.

He can open to where some conceit of mercy
moves with grace through a page or so

and point to his name there.
He throws the books away before they bury him.

If he needs books he'll get fresh books.
He strips the walls of old representations.

He takes down the walls, airs the place out,
lets what reminds him of death remind him of death.

He pits one hour against the moment.
Now what can he do?

Finishing a bottle of wine on the porch,
he stands, squares his shoulders,

carries his head up the mountain trail,
through the dogwood and scrub oak

toward the wild roses, stops along the way,
too sleepy to go on, and lies in the ivy to doze.

RED DIRT

—for Jerry

Then I run into Ruby,
the muse, that whore—
drunker than God
again, cruising
Larimer before gentrification,
when the bars have lemonade dispensers
with plastic domes spraying full
of forty-cent wine.

She's hanging off a parking meter
ugly as mud,
with her *duende* exposed,
having a very important
point, and I kiss her
with my tongue
the way I once tasted a shriveled apple
from Yeats's tree
at Thoor Ballylee.

IV

WHAT WAKES WITH MUSIC: TO THE MUSE

—for Whitney

Then it's loose,
breathy—
close and hot,
ragged, common folk
song in the lay of the
lowland, delta blue
tune and you, you
sound like free
jazz in the rusty bicycle
gaining on traffic on Louisville,
xenophobes on xylophones, bass lines
fouled on waste drums, crack
of rim shot, flash of crack
pipe in playground slam-dunk
black-on-black drive-by,
a cool TV-blue
tonality shuddering windows,
and you, your alluvial flair
infusing a slow air,
shabby strip malls, aluminum
pre-fab, pot-holed highways
with no shoulders to lean on,
and on down the riverbank,
white perch gulping dead air
of the paper mill, mercurial
in the sun and fire ants
filing over the levee—they'll
clean your bones
if you let them.

You'd think any moment
the mewling of bottleneck-guitar
would unearth from the riverbank,
fossilized ivories crawfish up
in bright glissandi—you'd
think there'd be a sign

of township jive rising in Southside,
some scrap of field-holler rhythm
revived or work song sung or moan
a-moanin' in a churchyard, some poor
soul visited by you—you'd
think you'd hear muted brass
in earth tones, in low throb
of slackwater, a listless
stealing back to that same ol'
used to be, something loose, breathy,
hot—I mean, semi-tropical
hot-damn jazz treatment
of forgotten folk
song, my darling
Clementine softly
behind the veil
of humidity hanging out
over the Ouachita, perfume-heavy
notes, magnolias the size of
childrens' faces, drooping in the heat.
One falls to the river, lost
and gone forever. What a plunge
in octaves, lingering a long time
on the *dreadful sorry* phrase.

What wakes with music
wakes the muse,
you, your
deep sorrow in the quick,
hotter now, tropical god-damned
purgatorial, breathless, high-toned
interpretation of hymns,
cicadas doing metal on the saw,
heavy metal, I mean lead, legacy
of a nation turned out
to be *this*—base
river, blocked
artery, ruined course
of the family
life nobody
said would turn out

to be this, man falling
down beat drunk
in the parking lot
heat, a woman fussing at him
drunkenly, smoking, about to burst
into flames, lost
and gone forever, dreadful sorry.

* * *

I shouldn't call it exile,
though once I saw where I came from,
my mother asleep in the heat.
I knew I'd had gills and had swum
out of the grail, never to return.
Once the sea advanced
and withdrew in music
where I was raised
and lowered to my feet
in the surge of foam,
and you, you were promised
in that people and land of color
grounded with the edible root
waves reclaimed and surrendered,
the scent of sea lettuce and laver
in froth of wind-torn crests of swells
and swells beyond, your muted fog
horn bluing my boyhood
two orchards inland, your apple
blossoms from the other world
blaring. You were so bright,
windows on five sides
of you, the lighthouse
keeper with your watchful
eye, so bright to have receded,
faded, golden on my skin, green
in the wind, gone before me,
dreadful sorry.

A rake and a rambling boy,
your face in my still waters,

the loud flower narcissus
in ten thousand mirrors
on the hillside, I followed
my footsteps, reckoning
and reckoning by heart
that ribbon of highway,
and by turning and turning,
came out all right, wound up
where I know I am, on South Grand
along the river, deep in the South,
a stray Quaker folk song and seven
deadly sins, fifteen jugglers,
five believers, twelve bars of blues
rephrasing fourteen stations of the cross,
too many hopeless romantics and
I don't know how many Zen buddhists
with a light bulb, waiting between the gins
and the evangelicals, between the ass
and the hole in the ground, waiting
for the reinvention of America,
waiting for the mincing little minuet
to release the hips and reinvent something,
waiting for good tunes to make us move
and for us to be so moved
to get up and shake it.
What wakes with music
wakes the muse.

* * *

Away across the river in soft cotton
shredded to the knees by briars,
thistles, burdock, mean-looking,
unaccommodating barbed-wire flora
with teeth, you stirred
these evanescent airs,
and a crescent icicle, Isis moon
tattooed on the blue, rose red
above the bosom of Abraham
in the land of cotton, and crossed
stars made a map of the four directions
I'd rambled like a folk song.

72

I wait at the river bridge
to hallelujah cross over
to the other side—
but the light says *red,*
and I wait. Tell me how long?
The river is gospel sung out
to the delta, song of Solomon
to mound of Venus, catfishy musk
of gumbo mud. I wait, looking
sidelong, and the light says
red, and I wait. I hesitate.
If I look sidelong
long enough I see zombies
taking over the bathhouse
at city pool, banging up cabañas,
roasting goats doused in dark rum,
smoke rising from their fire pits.
They're digging in.
They're establishing credit,
taking wives, their accountants
talking over coffee in styrofoam cups,
plans for aircraft, viaducts going up,
fences to guard the slackwater
where the exhausted may no longer come
to spawn, where I had lain and listened
to the bottom line in your breast.
The married-with-diamond belles,
sleeping with zombies now,
pose before their portraits
in mirrors over mantles,
eyeing the yardmen rise tall
and dark in the roses, black eggs
of the paddlefish cupped in hand
for the black market. I see buildings
with their windows, the emptiness
of lots, roads that might cross
uprooted and strewn, awash, then landless
undoing. The light says *red*
and I say *fuck it.* I'm gone. O
rock-a-my-soul. I wade in the water,

waving my axe—remember me, the guy
who danced through plate glass for you?
You'd think that would be enough,
marred with sweet confusion,
errant waves
and particles mixing it up down
in a deep depression in a
hard place and a rock my soul,
fractured neon all over me, shards
of the glitzy love between matter and energy,
a deer stuck in light, eyeballs locked
in fresh examples of the particularly
blasted landscapes you get down here,
a corny sense of nowhere to go
as a kind of groove, the way
Maceo Parker gets out front with the alto
and James Brown could be singing
any-damn-thing. No words for this
crossing—I want instead to vibrate
a reed, bees wings for a tongue,
back up slow as cane syrup
and strum up some pluck-
the-hesitation-out-of-me,
scat or bebop or trade fours
with the unconscious double,
get in a groove and stay there, airborne, wordless,
because it seems now that the Word
is a second-generation thing, a blank full
of adjectives, a vacancy kept
occupied by management—listen
to how we come down
to some abstract cave-man
power-and-control freak
speaking the truth
at us. Some mastodon
shadow darkens the mouth
of the cave, a thunderbolt
from a cyclops eye
nails the brainpan
to the frontal lobe,
and this Neanderthal

gentleman comes out
with a word about it
to protect his property.
There is no word, sing the songs—
no property. There is music
reinventing itself, flowing
toward the mouth, opening
and spilling mud, accretions
of clay. I see an image:
Bird on levee inventing *Ornithology.*

I see Whitman in his horse-drawn
work-wagon, aria swelling
in marsh grass about to be littered
with fallen leaves and limbs and
whiskey bottles and the worn
teeth of saws; and Garcia Lorca, alive
in flames of flamenco, shot through
the moon of parchment. You visited
Leadbelly in prison, or how would he
have gotten free? And Blake
and Blind Blake and "Blake-light
tragedy among the scholars
of war;" the bebop line
Ginsberg got from Kerouac got
from Bird, and Bird flying
through the eye of the needle.

Dead men moan, rooster crow,
something tell me I gotta go.

Bare feet flat on the other shore,
make me a pallet on your floor.

I see the hoochie coochie man,
the back door man.
I see the hoodoo man,
the jelly roll man.
I see Highway 51,
the seventh son,
the wang dang doodle,

the ditty wah ditty.
the little red rooster,
the midnight special—

I see Whitman—he's in a groove,
Jones, reinventing America. He says,
Can a match box hold your clothes?
He says, *Can somebody tell me*
what ditty wah ditty means?
I see mud people, tricksters, queers, Wobblies,
Tito Puente, black Baptists, black sopranos,
barbecue joints, black Cadillacs, blue notes,
funky barefoot folks shakin' everything they got,
and they're dong the mambo down below,
the funky chicken, a twisted version
of the Maypole dance. I see Federico
among the gypsy fires, sketching stage sets,
Allen watching the breath with the moon swelling
in his mudra around the omphalos.
"What peaches and What penumbras!"
What do you think was moiling in that ancient
connection with the starry dynamo? The groove,
Jim, the bebop whitey couldn't steal.
Whitman intones the first line
of American poetry: *I sing*, he says—listen:
I sing. Everyone in earshot rises
as if it is the result of some alignment
of planets, a stray *Star* card from the tarot
blows down from Grenada and lights
at five in the afternoon, at five
in the afternoon the waiter wraps the apron
as a ceremonial sash, brings fried fresh anchovies
in a basket, a plate of olives in oil,
a glass of oloroso to the woman with her cakes
of figs and wild fennel. In the shadow
he slips her the hotel key and winks,
at exactly five in the afternoon, in a minor plaza,
square, mall, common, green, bedazzled with red,
ribbons, *pícaros,* Whitman is singing,
and in a minor key, *la guitarra,* a lap-steel,
cello, accordion, elbow pipes, Stratocaster,

blues harp, bandonéon, penny whistle,
and over in Jersey seniors foxtrot on the night
boardwalk to a band of seniors, the trumpet
player leaning toward tattered and threadbare,
saintly, sweet light falling on an arbor
of plum tomatoes in Paterson, and near
a small cafe a couple dances a fandango,
edges soft with wine, and the great prostitute
La Petenera dies, and the streets aren't big enough
to contain the mourners, and the flamenco turns
from this *cancion* to *serranas,* for longing, yearning
to turn deeper to *sequiriyas,* for death and pain,
sound so heavy what should properly remain
transparent, ephemeral, abstract and bloodless
turns up stained with chili about the undershirt
and fixed up nice for the salsa club
and decked with dreadlocks on the 1 train
and reading the Korean news on the park bench
and busing in from Jersey to catch Sonny Rollins
at the West End, and in the shadow
of the el between the Third World
Cafe and two Vietnamese women squatting outside
their fish market, a kid in a groove
on tin-can-and-bucket drums, and behind him,
through refractions of glass, Ethiopians
scooping lentils with that flat spongy bread,
the Reverend Doctor Martin Luther King
Boulevard aglow with One-Hundred-and-Twenty-
Fifth-Street campfires, smoke above
the Tigris—I mean, this is far-reaching
jazz—I mean, let the shadows take over
downtown, give up the riverbanks
so big clarinets might be erected.
It would be good to rock the G.W. Bridge
with Federico's "Fistful of ants"
in his *Poet in New York* in his passion
for which he was murdered in his dream
of statuary, lambs and his assassination,
the perfect Italian tenor singing
from the Palisades. The gypsy girl
handles the fretless bass, lit by

the light of her unselfconsciousness.
A noisy motorbike turns the corner
in the stink of diesel and sweetness
of patchouli and hashish from Morocco
and orange blossoms and sugared almonds
cooking in oil. A tree blooms
in the Lower East Side
as if in a child's painting
of a Jewish deli. Jasmine hanging
from balconies turns the heads of the blind
from the blind school, old Castellanos
down in Adalucía for the sun
clap hands, and there's more sherry
than we all can drink, and you'd think this
would be enough, but the dark one—
the long Moroccan scarf three, four
times 'round her neck—
she lets the shoulder strap fall
in the shadow. In inverse prayer
she shoves her hands
between her thighs. Look
at the hole
he burned into his
arm for her!

ABOUT THE AUTHOR

William Ryan was born in New Jersey, but spent many years in Colorado and Massachusetts. His previous publications include *Dr. Excitement's Elixer of Longevity* (Donald Fine, Inc.), a novel, and *Eating The Heart Of The Enemy* (Lynx House), poems. He has won two Fellowships from the New Jersey Council on the Arts, and a number of prizes for individual poems. He lives in Monroe, Louisiana, and teaches creative writing and literature at Northeast Louisiana State University.